684040946686

KU-209-123

WITHDRAWN FROM STOCK

Inventors and Inventions

Level 11 – Lime

BookLife
Readers

Helpful Hints for Reading at Home

The graphemes (written letters) and phonemes (units of sound) used throughout this series are aligned with Letters and Sounds. This offers a consistent approach to learning whether reading at home or in the classroom.

HERE ARE SOME COMMON WORDS THAT YOUR CHILD MIGHT FIND TRICKY:

water	where	would	know	thought	through	couldn't
laughed	eyes	once	we're	school	can't	our

TOP TIPS FOR HELPING YOUR CHILD TO READ:

- Encourage your child to read aloud as well as silently to themselves.
- Allow your child time to absorb the text and make comments.
- Ask simple questions about the text to assess understanding.
- Encourage your child to clarify the meaning of new vocabulary.

This book focuses on developing independence, fluency and comprehension. It is a Lime level 11 book band.

©2022 **BookLife Publishing Ltd.**
King's Lynn, Norfolk PE30 4LS

ISBN 978-1-80155-115-1

All rights reserved. Printed in Poland.
A catalogue record for this book is available from the British Library.

Inventors and Inventions
Written by Joanna Brundle
Adapted by William Anthony
Designed by Gareth Liddington

Image Credits Images are courtesy of Shutterstock.com. With thanks to Getty Images, Thinkstock Photo and iStockphoto. Cover – lassedesign, Kwirry, MSSA, sraphotohut, Studio_G. p4–5 –Fasttailwind, Kokhanchikov. p6–7 –Alison restrepo quiroga, James S. Davis.. p8–9 – Kaca Skokanova. p10–11 – Feng Yu, HDesert. p12–13 – Glen Bowman, Tiger Images. p14–15 –metamorworks, drserg. p16–17 – ifong, A Daily Odyssey, Daniel Brasil. p18–19 – Avery Slack, Steve Mann. p20–21 – Juan Ci, Pangog200.

Contents

Page 4   Inventors and Inventions

Page 6   Famous Inventors

Page 8   Moving Around

Page 10   At Home

Page 12   Chocolate

Page 14   The Internet

Page 16   Lucky Accidents

Page 18   Weird and Wacky

Page 20   Young Inventors

Page 22   Index

Page 23   Questions

Inventors and Inventions

Inventions are completely new things. The people who have the ideas and create these inventions are called inventors. Some inventions make our lives easier. Others keep us safe or help us to keep in touch with one another.

Almost everything you see, from paper to computers, has been invented by someone who had a clever idea.

People have been inventing things for thousands of years. For example, the ancient Romans invented a type of heating for houses, and wigs were invented by the ancient Egyptians!

Some inventors spend a very long time working on their ideas. James Dyson took 15 years and thousands of attempts to make a vacuum cleaner that was good enough to sell.

Famous Inventors

Some inventors stand out from the rest because of their brilliant inventions because they invented so many things.

Leonardo da Vinci invented lots of incredible machines. In 1495 it's thought that he may have built a type of robot knight. He also thought of a machine like a helicopter, hundreds of years before the helicopter was invented.

Grace Hopper was an American mathematician and part of the US Navy. Hopper invented some clever technology that let computers understand different instructions. This changed how computers worked forever. Hopper also helped make the first ever computer that you could buy in shops. It was called UNIVAC I.

Moving Around

Have you ever thought about how your bicycle was invented? At the end of the 1800s, inventor James Starley created a type of penny-farthing bicycle. Penny-farthings had large front wheels and small back wheels. After the penny-farthing, Starley's nephew invented the 'safety bicycle', with two wheels that were the same size. Lighter mountain bikes were invented in the 1970s.

Penny farthing

Some inventions have made cars safer. Windscreen wipers were invented in 1903 by Mary Anderson. The idea came to her on a snowy car journey when her driver had to keep stopping to clear snow from the screen.

Garrett Morgan

Garrett Morgan invented traffic lights th use three lights. This made driving much sa

At Home

Have you ever tried to walk around your house in the dark? If so, you will understand why the invention of the light bulb was so important! In 1879, Thomas Edison perfected the light bulb. It was bright and lasted a long time.

Before light bulbs were invented, many people used candles or oil lamps to see in the dark.

In 1947, Valerie Hunter Gordon began making nappies that could be thrown away for her own children. She used cotton wool with a cover made from old nylon parachutes. Her idea was developed in the 1950s and her nappies soon went on sale.

In 1775, Alexander Cumming invented the first modern flushing toilet. It kept water in the toilet bowl to block nasty smells.

Chocolate

Did you know that chocolate was only a drink before it became a sweet snack? In 1847, Joseph Fry invented something that is still loved today. He mixed sugar with cocoa butter and cocoa powder and pressed the mixture into moulds to set. These became the first chocolate bars.

Chocolate chip cookies are a very tasty snack. But did you know they were invented by accident? In 1938, Ruth Wakefield had run out of cocoa powder while making chocolate cookies. Instead, she used broken chunks of chocolate. The short baking time meant that the chunks did not melt, and she had accidentally invented chocolate chip cookies!

The Internet

A group of computers all linked together is called a network. The internet is a giant network of computers that are linked to each other and share information. It began in 1969 as a network of just four computers in the United States, called ARPANET.

The first email was sent using ARPANET in 1971.

Computer scientist Tim Berners-Lee realised that a worldwide network of computers would let people around the world connect with each other. He invented something to help computers share information. His invention became known as the World Wide Web. This is what the 'www' stands for in web addresses.

Tim Berners-Lee

Lucky Accidents

Cornflakes were invented when John and Will Kellogg accidentally left boiled wheat to go stale. Instead of wasting it, they passed it through machines called rollers, hoping to make dough. Instead, they accidentally made flakes. They then tried again with other grains, including corn. The corn flakes became very popular.

George de Mestral invented Velcro in 1955, after a lucky accident. The prickly heads of certain plants had got stuck on his trousers and in his dog's fur during a walk. After looking closely at the hooks on the plants, he invented a hook and loop fastener for fabrics, which we now call Velcro.

Hooks on a plant

Hooks on Velcro

Weird and Wacky

Some inventions are very clever and can change lots of people's lives. Other inventions are simply weird and wacky! The Man from Mars Radio Hat was designed in 1949 by Victor Hoeflich. In the days before portable speakers, this hat let the person wearing it listen to music on the radio anywhere.

THE RADIO HAT
SEE NEW DESIGN

The Anti-theft Lunch Bag is a clear plastic bag printed with a picture of mould on it. It makes the sandwich inside look mouldy so that nobody will want to steal it!

The Sinclair C5 was like a car, but for just one person. It was a big failure because it didn't protect anyone from wind or rain, and people did not feel safe driving it.

Young Inventors

Many inventions were created by young people. Louis Braille was blind from a young age. This meant he could not see. When he was 15, he invented a way of reading and writing called braille. Braille uses six bumps in different patterns to mean different letters. A person uses their fingertips to feel the dots and read.

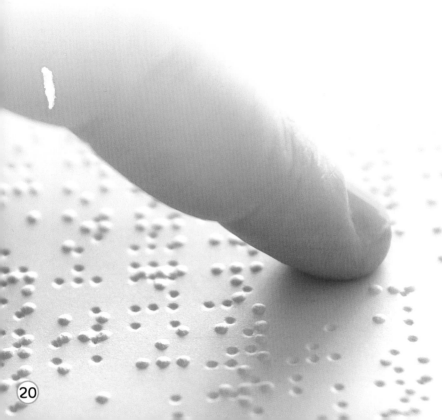

Deepika Kurup was born in 1998. She invented a way to clean water using a material that uses sunlight to make water safer to drink. Her invention doesn't cost too much money to use. This means it could bring clean drinking water to people all around the world.

Deepika Kurup

Index

ancient Egyptians 5

ancient Romans 5

bicycles 8

cars 9, 19

clothes 17

computers 4, 7, 14–15

food 12–13, 16, 19

robots 6

teenagers 20–21

toilets 11

How to Use an Index

An index helps us to find information in a book. Each word has a set of page numbers. These page numbers are where you can find information about that word.

Page numbers

Example: balloons 5, <u>8–10</u>, 19

Important word

This means page 8, page 10, and all the pages in between. Here, it means pages 8, 9 and 10.

Questions

1. What is an invention?

2. What did Louis Braille invent?

3. Which type of chocolate was invented first: the drink or the snack?

4. Can you use the contents page to find information about inventions that happened by accident?

5. Can you use the index to find a page in the book about food?